Serene Horizons

Amalgamation of Poetries

Aahel Boral

Ukiyoto Publishing

All global publishing rights are held by

Ukiyoto Publishing

Published in 2025

Content Copyright © Aahel Boral
ISBN 9789367956076

All rights reserved.
No part of this publication may be reproduced, transmitted, or stored in a retrieval system, in any form by any means, electronic, mechanical, photocopying, recording or otherwise, without the prior permission of the publisher.

The moral rights of the author have been asserted.

This is a work of fiction. Names, characters, businesses, places, events, locales, and incidents are either the products of the author's imagination or used in a fictitious manner. Any resemblance to actual persons, living or dead, or actual events is purely coincidental.

This book is sold subject to the condition that it shall not by way of trade or otherwise, be lent, resold, hired out or otherwise circulated, without the publisher's prior consent, in any form of binding or cover other than that in which it is published.

www.ukiyoto.com

About the Author

Aahel Boral

For the past undisclosed number of years, **Aahel** has been a leisure-time writer. He lives in Calcutta, India, spending his idle hours in intertwining his thoughts into evocative word crafts of poetries. Aahel has completed his high school in the year 2024 and is an eighteen-year-old man. He is an Undergraduate student of Economics. Apart from being a writer, Aahel also takes part in being a public speaker, an anthology publisher, a music enthusiast, an athlete, and chef.

ACKNOWLEDGEMENT

I am deeply indebted to the Ukiyoto Publishing House for giving me the golden opportunity to publish my Manuscript. I am also grateful to Riddhima Di for her undulating support and guidance.

Thanks to my family and friends for being there by my side through the thick and thins.

SYNOPSIS

This poem collection is a conglomeration of poems catering to valid human emotions. It delves deeper into the id, ego and superego and takes a closer look at how we evolve as human beings with an active emotional repertoire.

CONTENTS

Nocturne	1
Celestial Divine	2
Canvas of Art	3
Lovesome Marine	4
Untold Tales	5
Nature of Disposition	6
Doomed Immortality	7
Eternal Love	8
Pilgrim of Peace	10
Just You and Me	11
A Beauty in Disguise	12
Chains of Oblivion	13
Infinite Sparks	14
The Limerick's Jest	15
Strangers of an Unsung Love	16
Blessed with Eternal Sleep	17
Ensō in Zen	18
The Uncaged Enchantment	19
What's Life?	20
Thorns of Treachery	21
Timeless Romance	22
Love-struck	23

Marrow of Sorrow	24
The Sea of Salvation	25
Forever Found	26
Love's Unyielding Vow	27
Words that were never written	28
Mirrors and Mist	29
Suspended	30
Fading Silence	31
Everlasting Love	32
A Teacher Within	33

Nocturne

I'd rather drown in your shadows,
Than swim in someone's light.
For in your dark,
I find the secrets, looming, soft and grim.
That sings a dirge, a melancholy spark.

Your shadows cloak me in a shroud of dreams,
Where sorrow dances with tender grace,
As I sink in the depths of muted screams,
I taste the bitter mirth of your embrace.

Oh, let me wander through your endless night,
Where moonlight castes its silver luminescence,
And stars, like poetry, adorn the sight,
Enchanting souls in fragile effervescence.

For in your shadows, beauty's tears do flow,
A sanctuary where my heart can grow.

Celestial Divine

Beneath your gaze,

A Galaxy unfurls…

A thousand stars,

Their brilliance swirls…

Each glance,

A constellation's art…

In your eyes,

I find my beating heart…

Canvas of Art

In the gallery of their shared dreams,
He remains her muse eternally…
Each colour and line a testament,
To a Love that defies all sentiment.
As in the dance of brush and heart,
Their story unfolds a canvas of art…

Lovesome Marine

You remind me of the ocean…

Deep and intense,

Powerful and sensitive,

Raging and Calm,

Steadfast and steady,

Crushing and receding.

With sunsets in your eyes,

And, sharks around your heart.

And, starfish in your soul…

Untold Tales

Some stories…

Scorched by fate's chains,

Remains unfinished…

While even the spot of time,

Slowly erases…

The ink from their pages…

Nature of Disposition

In the realm of obscure,

A Lygophile's delight,

And, in its charm…

Seraphic's dreams take a flight.

Acosmist's soul,

Amidst the chaos we roam…

Eccedentesiast's smile,

Hiding words unknown…

Doomed Immortality

As his eyes closed for the final time,
She realized,
Even the darkest hearts,
Can find redemption in light of Love.
And, with his last breath,
The immortality became a curse,
For Eternity…
And, an endless life of pain,
Was his sentence for loving her…

Eternal Love

In the twilight's embrace, our love was born,
A pure and tender flame forever sworn.
Two souls entwined, like stars above,
We basked in the warmth of Eternal Love

With whispering winds, we danced as one,
Our hearts, a symphony, in unison.
No bounds or barriers, our love would know,
United by fate, in harmony we'd grow.

Like roses, our love bloomed with sweet delight,
Each day, a blissful dream, a shining light.
Through life's trials, we'd face hand in hand,
Guided by love's compass, we would withstand.

In your embrace, each moment feels divine,
Every touch, like heaven, oh how it's sublime.
Your smile, infectious, brightens each day,
You are my sun, chasing all darkness away.

Through ages, our love will forever be,
An unbreakable bond, for eternity.
Wrapped in your love, in every breath I take,
With you, my love, I've found my soul's true mate.

So let our love soar, like eagles high above,
Defying time, as we embrace eternal love.
Forever entwined, forever intertwined,
Our love, an immortal legacy, we'll find.

Pilgrim of Peace

The ears were all dripped,
In the crimson phonic symphony,
Of screams of hopelessness…
I saw harbingers of peace,
Carrying the stabbed endeavors,
Of Peace and Hope…

Just You and Me

Oh! I could fall for you again.
My stuttering, you're the cause,
Your eyes, a constellation's art…
Holding hands on serene nights,
Let time pause,
Let our silences speak,
I wish for an eternity,
For another seven lives,
And, a hundred more.
Just like this, you and me…

A Beauty in Disguise

She is not just a whisper of potential,
But, a roar of capability.
Within her beats the heart of a warrior,
The soul of a dreamer,
And, the strength of thousand lifetimes.
Her dreams are not mere wishes,
But, the seeds of change.
Let her rise…
Unshackled and unafraid,
For she is the embodiment of resilience,
And, the essence of possibility…

Chains of Oblivion

In the Shadows cast,
The chains do bind…
Your fate is entwined,
And, escape declined…
The darkness calls,
Your will it breaks…
As Hell's embrace,
Your soul it takes…
Beware…!
It's the Chains of Oblivion…

Infinite Sparks

Infinite Sparks,
Ignite my nimble quill,
Setting free the dreams,
That hides within my mind…
Like fairies dancing,
On the window sill,
Enchanting the world,
With their tales intertwined…

The Limerick's Jest

The Limerick's Jest,

A fleeting disguise.

Masking the pain,

Despite its tries.

For beneath the wit,

Seriousness lies.

In this moonlight's serenade,

Mournful guise…

Strangers of an Unsung Love

As the ink of passion dried out,
Love was lost yet again.
And in the end,
We both were blind.
She never saw me,
I never saw someone like her,
But, the moon,
And, the moon became someone else's star…
It ended…
Yes, it ended…
One life became two.

Leaving few lines empty,
Just in case,
Two strangers meet again…

Blessed with Eternal Sleep

As I am growing cold,
Abandoning something behind…
Leaving the shore,
Which was there beneath me,
Now it is not mine.
Wish I could reach my pilot's cockpit,
Without any dither.
Heavenly almighty…
Thanks for giving the inevitable blessings,
As I receive it with my vague hands…

Ensō in Zen

In the end, when no one stood by his side,
He couldn't help, but think,
How poetic it was,
That he had landed in such a predicament.
Throughout his life,
He was afraid of being forgotten,
Of being left alone.
He had led himself to believe,
His life had actually come to full circle.

The Uncaged Enchantment

In my poetic playground,
Mirth shall bloom.
As metaphors entwine,
Like playful vines,
Silent whispers dance,
Banishing all gloom.
With rhymes,
That twist and turn like winding lines.
Let's paint a scene,
With strokes of playful hues,
Where words are merry jester on the stage.
On the strings of verse,
Imagination strews,
An endless carnival, uncaged…

What's Life?

There is a worst thing about stories…
They have no end.
Sometime, somewhere, somehow…
And, in the end,
You're left with only one question,
"How?"
Feels like "Didn't the story just begin?"
My friend,
That's Life…

Thorns of Treachery

Walking cautiously among thorns,
While I have endured wounds from flowers.
You speak of stranger's tales,
Yet, I've faced trials from my own.
All the wounds upon my heart,
Are from deemed as friends…

Timeless Romance

In lifetimes past, we wandered, our hearts entwined,
Where Love laid claim to beat and breath,
A cosmic dance that spun beyond the mind,
Our souls entangled through each birth and death.
In every life, the furnace of our fire,
Burnt bright and fierce, a testament to fate,
Yet cruelly snuffed before our sweet desire,
Could finally bloom, and thus we'd separate.
Yet there's always been,
A Timeless Romance through her eyes…

Love-struck

In your absence, I invent you,
First thought at dawn, last before sleep.
We're silent, yet we understand,
Our hearts in harmony.
My words may be imperfect,
But my emotions are genuine and true.
You fill my heart with rhythm,
Making me whole.
Dear Love,
I won't stop waiting for you…

Marrow of Sorrow

I bled in the dark, where Love was a knife,
Cutting through marrow, searing my life,
I clung to the shards of shattered embrace,
Each kiss a bruise with a touch of disgrace.
The weight of her words, jagged and cold,
Burrowed like fire through cracks in my soul.
I screamed in silence, my heart torn in two,
Drowning in promises that never were true.

The Sea of Salvation

In times of despair,
When the fields are covered by bodies,
And, oceans filled with blood,
The Son of God will descend,
To protect his children.
The Heavens shout out in glory,
And, the Heathens begin to worry.
My Lord,
It's the Sea of Salvation.

Forever Found

In every life, we've known the better sting,
Of Love's sweet promise ripped away too soon,
But still we rise, a phoenix on the wing,
To chase the whisper of a long-lost tune.
No matter where or when our souls may roam,
In every life, we'll always find each other,
Our Home…

Love's Unyielding Vow

The pages of my heart, inked with your essence,
Are bound by the thread of Love's eternal dance,
A devotion that transcends life quintessence,
And frees our souls,
To hope, to yearn, to glance.
Through the hands of time may tear us asunder,
Our Love's a beacon that will guide me through,
And in each life, I will search and wander,
Until I find my way once more to you.
In the face of time's cruel, unending trial,
I vow to love you through every fateful mile.

Words that were never written

Ornamented with gold and platinum,
Craftsmanship of Heaven,
But poorly interwoven,
Words that were never written…

Worthy of unexpected coronation,
Intertwined with administration,
Alas! The fractured aspiration,
Words that were never written…

Now, the dwell inside me for habitation,
Buried in the depths of unconsciousness,
Forming a tumor for Salvation,
They will die with my annihilation,
Words that were never ever written…

Mirrors and Mist

I saw God in morning mist.
She whispered the lies of my ancestors,
Opening my eyes into a world of wonder.
Is my life mine, or one with the world?
If we meet in the past,
Would we have a future?
Darkness surrounds us,
As the world implodes,
And, God hangs from Satan's noose.

Suspended

It is cold in here,
And, the only colour I can see,
Comes from the red,
Dripping down my back,
And, the holograms fogging my eyes.
The only thing that I can feel
Are the chains cutting into my wrists,
And, the only thing I can hear,
The Slackening of my Heart…

Fading Silence

Some nights, the dark grows jagged and wild,
A hunger, a weight I can't seem to lift.
My dreams dance through its endless aisles,
And, I'm the prey to their twisted gift.
Tonight is one of those nights,
They claw; they tear at the seams of my fragile mind.
I clutch at my breath; I count every flow.
The silence between us feels cruel, unkind.
I think of her name, where her voice might be,
I could call her, though its painfully late…

Everlasting Love

A Journal's pages, brittle and worn,
Tells of our Love that bloomed in distant lands,
As a Soldier and his bride, Love forlorn,
Fate's cruel hand would sever ours,
In the next life, a painter and his muse,
A Masterwork of passion and despair,
Our Love's intensity no canvas could diffuse,
Yet death would once again,
Our Bond impair…

A Teacher Within

In the dwelling of the heart, a guest house stands,
Where travellers from realm of feelings land,
Each day a visitor, a lesson anew,
In this abode of soul, life's tapestry weaves through.

Welcome them all, the joy and the despair,
The laughter and tears, the love and the scare,
With open arms greet them, for they are your guide,
In this inn of existence, emotions reside.

Some guests arrive with a radiant smile,
Their presence like sunlight, hearts they beguile,
Dance with them, for they light up the room,
In their embrace, the blossoms of hope bloom.

Some come as shadows, draped in sorrow's veil,
Their whispers of sadness, a mournful tale,
Sit with them, let their stories unfold,
In the arms of grief, wisdom takes hold.

Others arrive like a tempestuous storm,

Raging within, their passions transform,
Face them head on, the winds of desire,
In the heart of the fire, the phoenix aspires.

Some glide in gently, like a soft, tender breeze,
Their touch, a soothing balm, hearts they appease,
Rest in their presence, let serenity seep,
In the quiet moments, secrets they keep.

In this guest house, a gathering of life's hues,
Each visitor a teacher, a mirror for truths,
Treasure them all, the bitter and the sweet,
In their embrace, the heart's rhythm we meet.

And remember, dear soul, in this sacred space,
You are never alone, as you journey with grace,
Each guest a friend, a mentor, a home,
In the guest house of being, love's essence is known.

.

www.ingramcontent.com/pod-product-compliance
Lightning Source LLC
LaVergne TN
LVHW050032090526
838199LV00126B/3496